Speaking Test Preparation Pack for
First Certificate in English

Acknowledgements

Cambridge ESOL is grateful to the following for permission to reproduce photographs:

Part 2

Making music: Corbis for musicians playing traditional instruments and family making music at home.

Educational visits: National Trust Photo Library for schoolchildren on visit to farm.

Every effort has been made to identify the copyright owners for material used, but it is not always possible to identify the source or contact the copyright holders. In such cases, Cambridge ESOL would welcome information from the copyright owners.

University of Cambridge ESOL Examinations
1 Hills Road
Cambridge
CB1 2EU
UK

www.CambridgeESOL.org

First published 2008
Printed in the United Kingdom by Cambridge Printing Services Ltd
ISBN 978-1-906438-38-8

Contents

Teacher's Notes

Student Worksheets

Introduction

This *Speaking Test Preparation Pack for FCE* has been specially created to help you prepare your students for the Speaking test of the First Certificate in English (FCE) from Cambridge ESOL. Written by experienced Speaking test examiners, it consists of:

- a book containing comprehensive Teacher's Notes and a set of six Student Worksheets which provide detailed practice for all parts of the FCE Speaking test
- one set of candidate visuals in colour to allow you and your students to practise with realistic visual stimulus
- a DVD showing real students taking a Speaking test to give your students a clear idea of what to expect on the day.

The Student Worksheets can be photocopied to use in class, or printed from the files on the DVD if you prefer. Worksheets 1–4 cover the four parts of the Speaking test in detail and contain a variety of exercises and discussion tasks using the video on the DVD. The Introductory Worksheet is designed to give students an overview of the whole Speaking test and the Supplementary Worksheet covers how the Speaking test is assessed.

The Teacher's Notes for each worksheet explain in detail how to conduct each activity and provide answers to and commentary on the various exercises. There are also 'Teaching Tips' for each of the four main worksheets, giving you extra ideas for use in class, and 'Helpful Hints for Students' with useful advice for you to pass on.

The DVD contains video of one complete FCE Speaking test for you to use with the worksheets and electronic versions of the Student Worksheets and candidate visuals.

We hope you enjoy using the *Speaking Test Preparation Pack for FCE* and wish your students every success when they take the test.

Cambridge ESOL

FCE Speaking test
Teacher's Notes

■ Aims of the DVD and worksheets

- to raise students' awareness of the format of the FCE Speaking test
- to focus students' attention on techniques that will improve their performance
- to provide opportunities for students to practise the language used in the different parts of the test
- to update teachers on the current test format for the FCE Speaking test
- to provide activities and teaching tips for teachers to use with examination classes.

Please note:

The DVD and worksheets are not intended as a forum for discussing grades. Although in certain questions we are asking students to look at the candidates' performance, it is with a view to improving the students' own performance and not for them to grade the candidates on the DVD.

The FCE Speaking test on the DVD has been produced for teaching purposes only and is not a live exam. There are, therefore, no grades available.

■ How to use the DVD and worksheets

The Student Worksheets are at the back of this book in the section beginning on page 25. The tasks in the worksheets are to be used at your discretion to create maximum benefit for your students. The guidelines below are suggestions only.

You can use the worksheets to:
- introduce the FCE Speaking test at the beginning of your course
- review or revise key points near the exam date
- focus on different parts of the test at different times according to your syllabus.

Please note:

The material is not designed to be used as complete lessons of any fixed length. Make sure that your students are aware when the answers to the tasks cannot be found on the DVD.

Some of your students may find these activities challenging. If necessary, adapt or simplify the tasks and give assistance where needed.

Student's Introductory Worksheet

■ Task One: general information about the FCE Speaking test

Ask the students to fill in the missing information on the worksheet. Tell them they can find some of the information they need on the Candidate Support site at
www.candidates.CambridgeESOL.org/cs/Help_with_exams/General_English/FCE
and in the *Information for Candidates* booklet which they can download.

Answers

1. Length: _____**14**_____ minutes
2. Normal format: _____**2**_____ candidates and _____**2**_____ examiners
3. Number of parts: _____**4**_____
4. The Speaking test is worth _____**20**_____ % of the whole FCE exam (all papers).

■ Task Two: what happens in the FCE Speaking test

Ask the students to complete the table on the worksheet with the correct information from the box below.

• leads a discussion • exchanges views and opinions • asks individual direct questions	• expresses opinions through comparing • gives personal information • initiates discussion

Answers

Parts	Timing	What the interlocutor does	What a candidate does	Possible range of language used
1. Interview	3 minutes	**asks individual direct questions**	**gives personal information**	General interactional and social language: • giving personal information about everyday circumstances • expressing opinions about everyday life
2. Individual long turn	4 minutes	asks each candidate to talk about two visuals for 1 minute	**expresses opinions through comparing**	Organising a larger unit of discourse: • comparing • describing • expressing opinions
3. Collaborative task	3 minutes	asks candidates to talk together using visual prompts	exchanges ideas and opinions, makes suggestions, agrees, disagrees, and **initiates discussion**	Sustaining an interaction: • exchanging ideas • expressing and justifying opinions • agreeing and/or disagreeing • suggesting • speculating • evaluating • decision-making through negotiating
4. Discussion on topics related to Part 3	4 minutes	**leads a discussion**	**exchanges views and opinions**	• expressing and justifying opinions • agreeing and/or disagreeing

■ Task Three: about the FCE Speaking test

Ask the students to read the statements and write 'True' or 'False' next to each one.

Answers

1. You can choose to take the test in a pair or a group of three. – **FALSE**. However, if there is an odd number of candidates at the centre, the last test will be a group of three.
2. The assessor asks you questions during the test. – **FALSE**. The interlocutor asks the questions.
3. Only the assessor awards marks. – **FALSE**. The assessor gives detailed marks on grammar, vocabulary, discourse management, pronunciation and interactive communication but the interlocutor also gives a global mark.
4. You are given your marks at the end of the test. – **FALSE**. Examiners are not allowed to give any indication of a candidate's performance at the end of the test, and candidates should be discouraged from asking.
5. You might not know your partner. – **TRUE**. At open and devolved centres candidates may be paired at random.
6. You are not tested on your general knowledge. – **TRUE**. This is a test of language, not of general knowledge.
7. In Part 1, you ask your partner questions. – **FALSE**. You are asked direct questions by the interlocutor.
8. In Part 2, if your partner runs out of things to say you can help. – **FALSE**. Part 2 is the time when candidates can speak alone and uninterrupted.
9. The questions are written at the top of the page in Parts 2 and 3. – **TRUE**. The questions are written at the top of the page of visuals in the Candidate Booklet to help candidates remember and focus on the task.
10. You should interact with your partner in both Parts 3 and 4. – **TRUE**. It is important in Part 3 that candidates interact with each other, and in Part 4 the interlocutor may address a question to both candidates for them to discuss. It is also possible in Part 4 for a candidate to add something to what their partner has said.

 Tell the students to check their answers with a partner. Then play the DVD and tell them to check if they were right.

FCE Speaking test
Teacher's Notes

This worksheet is based on Part 1 of the FCE Speaking test.

■ Task One

1. Tell the students to work with a partner and ask and answer the questions in turn.
   * Where are you from?
   * What do you like about living in (partner's country/UK)?
   * Do you find it easy to study where you live? (Why?/Why not?)
   * Is there something you'd really like to learn about? (Why would you like to learn about it?)
   * Which area of (candidate's country) would you like to get to know better?
   * What's the most interesting place you've visited near here? (Why do you think it's interesting?)
   * How much TV do you watch in a week? (Do you think this is too much?) (Why?/Why not?)
   * Do you use the internet to learn new things? (What sort of things do you learn about?)

 2. Play Part 1 on the DVD. Ask the students to discuss how their answers were different from Ana's and Giallo's.

   Answers will depend on what the students say. Encourage them to think about how well they answered the questions, and how they feel about the candidates on the DVD.

■ Task Two

 1. Play Part 1 on the DVD again. Ask the students to make notes in the table on the worksheet.

   Answers

What does Ana say about . . .	*What does Giallo say about . . .*
Madrid when she answers question 1? We don't find out anything about Madrid at this point because the answer isn't extended, although it is not necessary to extend this answer.	*Perugia when he answers question 1?* Giallo extends his answer by explaining where in Italy Perugia is located.
Madrid when she answers question 2? Ana extends her answer well here. She tells us that Madrid is a very big city, one of the most important cities in Spain, that it's the capital and that there are lots of things to do there.	*living in the UK?* Giallo says he doesn't know if he likes living in the UK, but he still goes on to find positive things to say about the fact that English people are practical and organised. Even if candidates don't like something it's still important to go on to say why, and it's even better if they can still find a positive comment to make.
the area of her country she'd like to know better? Again Ana gives a full answer, explaining that she'd like to know more about the north of Spain but she is a bit 'lazy' about going there because she likes hot weather and the beach, and that this is a good area with old buildings and is interesting.	*studying?* Giallo could have said more in answer to this question but we still learn that he thinks it is 'too crowdy' at university and it was easier for him to learn at school.
the most interesting place she's visited? We learn that the place Ana finds interesting is London and that she has been there 3 or 4 times. However, Ana says very little about why it is the most interesting place for her. We find out only that it is a good city and very big.	*how much TV he watches?* Giallo answers the question confidently: he doesn't watch TV because he has the internet which he thinks is better but at home he watched TV for 50% of the day!
using the internet to learn new things? Ana says that she would like to learn new things on the internet but actually she doesn't. She uses the internet for communication with friends.	

2. Play Part 1 on the DVD again if necessary and ask the students to discuss the questions on the worksheet.

Answers

- Which questions do Giallo and Ana answer well? – Giallo answers all his questions well. He always answers confidently and goes on to give explanations for his answers. Ana gives a very full answer to her second question when she talks in detail about Madrid and she also gives an extended answer to the question about the area of her country she'd like to get to know better. Both students perform well in this part of the test.
- Which questions could they have answered better? – Giallo's answer to the question about living in the UK could have been better explained. We are unsure why Giallo thinks people in the UK are practical and organised, and what he means when he says that they 'move around'. He could also have gone into more detail on the question of studying. When answering her questions, Ana does not always fully explain why she says what she says, in particular in answering the question about London.
- Who do you think gave the best answers in Part 1 of the test? Why? – Giallo gave the best answers overall because he nearly always extended his answers and explained the reasons for what he said. When answering the Part 1 questions candidates should keep asking themselves 'Why?' so that they give full answers to all the questions. They should not, however, say more than would be expected in a normal conversation (i.e. no long prepared speeches).

■ Task Three

1. Ask the students to think of two questions to ask their partner in each of the topic areas.

   - sports
   - leisure interests
   - work and study
   - family

   - travel and holidays
   - entertainment
   - experiences
   - daily life

   - jobs/studies/education
   - the area where they live
   - likes and dislikes
   - future plans

2. Tell the students to practise in pairs or small groups, taking turns to ask and answer questions. Encourage them to extend their answers in an interesting way, and to use a range of grammar and interesting vocabulary. Remind them that this part requires personal answers and personal information and ideas.

1. Put aside time at the beginning or end of lessons to give students the chance to talk about themselves and their lives. Give them a general topic, for example 'What you do at the weekends' or 'Where you like to go shopping and what you buy' and give them time to discuss these topics in groups. Prepare lists of useful phrases that come up during these group discussions.

2. Put students into pairs and give them time to write questions on different topic areas related to their lives. Ask them to use a range of tenses when forming these questions. Students can then question each other. Monitor the students as they speak and give feedback on their performance.

3. Ask students to prepare a very short presentation on one aspect of their lives, for example, 'My plans for the future'. Students can then deliver this presentation in small groups while the other students think up three questions to ask. Monitor the students and give feedback.

4. Give students practice that involves using a range of tenses to ensure that they are able to talk about their past experiences, current situation and future plans.

Listen carefully to the questions you are asked. In this part of the test questions will be about who you are and what you do.

Don't be afraid to ask the interlocutor to repeat the question if you're not sure what you have to say. You won't lose any marks for doing this.

Don't prepare long answers before the test because this won't sound natural.

Listen to your partner's answers so that you can relate your answers to what he/she has said.

Speak clearly so that both examiners can hear you.

Try not to give very short answers to the questions. For example, if the interlocutor asks you about your plans for the future, try to say more than, 'I'd like to be a teacher'. Try to say 'I'd like to be a teacher because . . .' and then give one or two reasons why. Do this whenever you can.

Don't speak for too long. The examiner will let you know when you have to stop. This may be as a spoken instruction, for example 'thank you', or by gesture. Make sure you don't carry on speaking for longer than expected as you need to share the time with your partner.

This worksheet is based on Part 2 of the FCE Speaking test. Use the candidate visuals provided with this book or, before the lesson, print out the Part 2 photographs (preferably in colour) from the DVD and make sure you have enough copies to give one set to each pair of students.

■ Task One: focus on Ana

1. Play the beginning of Part 2 on the DVD and stop it after the interlocutor has given Ana her task. Tell the students to listen carefully to the interlocutor's instructions to Ana and write the missing information in the box on the worksheet.

   Answer

   > *Interlocutor:* Ana, it's your turn first. Here are your photographs. They show **people making music in different ways**.
   >
   > I'd like you to compare the photographs and say **why you think the music is important to the different groups of people**.

2. Ask the students what question they think the interlocutor will ask Giallo after Ana has spoken. Tell them to write it in the box on the worksheet.

3. Ask the students to work with a partner and take it in turns to do Ana's task. Tell them to discuss the questions on the worksheet.
   - Did you speak for a minute?
   - Did you compare two pictures in an organised way and answer the second part of the task?

4. Ask the students to watch Ana doing the task on the DVD but stop the recording after Ana's long turn and Giallo's response question. Ask the students to compare their performances with Ana's.

   Answers

   - Why does Ana find it hard to do this task? – Ana just compares the photos. She doesn't go on to do the second part of the task.

   Ask the students if they were right about Giallo's question.

   > *Interlocutor:* Giallo, **what type of music would you prefer to listen to?**

■ Task Two: focus on Giallo

1. Play the next part of Part 2 on the DVD. Tell the students to listen carefully to the interlocutor's instructions to Giallo and write the missing information in the box on the worksheet. Stop the DVD after the interlocutor has given Giallo his task.

   Answer

   > *Interlocutor:* Giallo, here are your photographs. They show **people of different ages on educational visits**.
   >
   > I'd like you to compare the photographs and say **what you think people will learn on their visits**.

2. Ask the students what question they think the interlocutor will ask Ana after Giallo has spoken. Tell them to write it in the box on the worksheet.

3. Ask the students to work with a partner and take it in turns to do Giallo's task. Tell them to discuss the questions on the worksheet.
   - Did you speak for a minute?
   - Did you remember to answer the second part of the task?
   - Did you look at the questions on your sheet to remind yourself of what you had to say?

   Check that the students managed to keep going and that they compared the pictures and went on to do the second part of the task. Remind students to read the task at the top of the page so that they know they are doing the right thing.

4. Ask the students to watch Giallo doing the task on the DVD. Ask them to compare their performances with his.

   Discuss the fact that Giallo answers both the first and the second part of the task.

   Ask the students if they were right about Ana's question.

   Answer

Interlocutor:	Ana, **which of these things would you like to learn about?**

■ Task Three

1. Play the whole of Part 2 again, and tell the students to complete the table on the worksheet.

   This will encourage students to see what Ana and Giallo did well and what they could have done better.

   Answers

What do they say . . .	Ana	Giallo
What do they say about the first picture?	a group of people from a foreign country playing music in the street/in fancy dress	some old people in a museum looking to a statue
What do they say about the second picture?	young people/family at home/playing music for fun	A group of people on an archaeological site/a guided tour. In a field/there's something important because the guide is pointing his finger to the ground.
What do they say when they compare the pictures?	The difference is that one is in the street and one is at home. Ana repeats herself because she has forgotten about the second part of the task.	Giallo doesn't compare the pictures with each other, he describes what he can see in each and uses comparison for the second part of the task. This is fine.
What do they say when they answer the second part of the task?	Ana does not answer the second part of the task and so runs out of things to say.	Giallo makes good use of comparison to deal with what he thinks people will learn on their visit: 'People will generally learn more on the first one because while in the museum you can see arts and exhibitions, I think that is more useful to learn than guided tour on the outside. In the second one we are not completely sure of what they are talking about so . . .'. Giallo compares the pictures when addressing the second part of the task. Giallo speaks for the full minute and is stopped by the interlocutor.
Do they give an appropriate response to the listening candidate question?	Ana says 'I think I would prefer the first picture in a museum because when you know more about art you enjoy more'. Ana's answer is appropriate: she says which picture she would prefer and briefly explains why.	Giallo says 'Well I'm into heavy metal and rock music'. His answer is short but appropriate. He is able to demonstrate his knowledge of colloquial language 'I'm into . . .'.

2. Ask the students to discuss the question on the worksheet.
   - Who does the task best, Ana or Giallo? (Why?)

   Answer

   Giallo, because he addresses both parts of the task and speaks for the full minute. Ana is unable to speak for the full minute because she relies only on what she can see in the pictures and forgets to deal with the second part of the task. This part of the task is now written at the top of the page in the Candidate Booklet to remind students of what they have to do in addition to comparing the pictures.

■ Useful phrases

Below are some useful phrases which may be helpful for students when comparing the photos, but students should take care not to overuse them.

Comparing and contrasting	Both of these . . . Neither of these . . . One of these . . . , while the other . . . This one . . . , but on the other hand that one . . . This picture . . . whereas the other . . .
Comparing	Both pictures . . . This picture . . . whereas this one . . .
Speculating	It's hard to say, but I think . . . It looks like a . . . I'd say . . . It must be . . . It might be . . . It could be . . . It can't be . . . I don't think it . . ., because . . .
Expressing opinions	Personally, I . . . I've never thought about it, but I suppose . . . I don't really like . . ., but if I had to choose . . . It seems to me that . . .

1. Ask students to find and bring pictures into class on a certain topic, for example 'Sport'. Get them to describe these pictures to each other in pairs but without showing each other the pictures. Students can then look at each other's pictures and comment on the descriptions given and what could have made the descriptions better.

2. Get students to time each other when they do Part 2 practice so that they are able to get a feel for how long a minute is when they have to keep talking on their own.

3. At this level a good way to deal with Part 2 is to get students to:
   - describe picture one (about 15 seconds)
   - compare it with picture two by finding similarities and differences (about 15 seconds)
   - address the second part of the task for each picture, continuing to find similarities and differences (about 30 seconds).

   If students are encouraged to think of Part 2 as being broken down in this way, they may feel more confident about speaking for the full minute.

4. Give students examples of Part 2 pairs of photographs. Get them to predict what they are going to be asked to say in the second part of the rubric. For example, if they are shown two holiday pictures they might guess that they have to 'say what the people are enjoying about the different holidays'. When they have made their predictions, give them 1 minute in pairs to find as many different responses as they can. This will give students practice in finding things to say quickly during the test itself.

Listen very carefully to the instructions, paying particular attention to the 'and say…' part of the task. Remember that this will be written above the photographs to remind you. You will need to answer this in order to keep going for the full minute and to use a good range of language.

Start speaking straight away, so that you make full use of the time allowed. You won't be given any extra time if you don't.

Say as much as you can about the first picture before you move on to the second. This will help you not to go backwards and forwards between the pictures and repeat yourself.

Don't worry if you don't know the word for something – paraphrase it.

And don't worry if the interlocutor stops you, this just means that you have spoken for the right amount of time, but do try not to stop until the interlocutor says 'thank you'!

Don't interrupt while your partner is talking. Even if your partner has difficulty finding things to say, you are not allowed to help during this part of the test.

Imagine that you have discussed all the similarities and differences in the photographs, and you have said for each photograph what the interlocutor has asked you to say, but the interlocutor still hasn't said 'thank you'. What do you do then? Go on to say, for example, which of the activities you would like to try or which of the two people you would like to be. It's important to try your best to keep talking for the full minute.

This worksheet is based on Part 3 of the FCE Speaking test. Use the candidate visuals provided with this book or, before the lesson, print out the Part 3 pictures (preferably in colour) from the DVD and make sure you have enough copies to give one set to each pair of students.

■ Task One

1. Play the beginning of Part 3 on the DVD. Tell the students to listen carefully to the interlocutor's instructions and write the missing information in the box on the worksheet.

Answer

> Interlocutor: Now I'd like you to talk about something together for about 3 minutes.
>
> I'd like you to imagine that a local café wants to attract more people. Here are some of the suggestions they're considering.
>
> First, talk to each other about **how successful these suggestions might be.** Then decide **which two would attract most people.**

2. Tell the students to work with a partner and do the task. Remind them to spend 3 minutes discussing all the pictures.

3. Ask the students to discuss the questions on the worksheet with a partner. When they have finished, answer any general questions they have about the task.
   • Did you have time to discuss all the pictures?
   • Did you have something to say about all the pictures?
   • Did you find any pictures easy or difficult to talk about?
   • Did you reach a decision too early and leave yourselves with nothing else to talk about?

4. Now play all of Part 3 on the DVD. Ask the students to compare their performances with Ana's and Giallo's.

■ Task Two

Play Part 3 on the DVD again. Ask the students to answer the questions on the worksheet.

Answers

1. Who starts the discussion and how? – Giallo. He starts the discussion but offers Ana the chance to speak: 'What do you think about that?'
2. Who responds the most and how? – Giallo responds most. Ana moves from one picture to the next, agreeing with Giallo but often without giving her own opinion.
3. Do they seem interested in each other and what they are saying? – Both students are sensitive to turn taking and don't interrupt each other. Giallo looks at Ana frequently and listens to what she has to say. Ana does this less frequently. She tends to look down at the pictures while Giallo is talking. When Giallo is talking about having tables outside she seems to be preparing her next question rather than listening to him and responding to what he has to say. She just says 'yeah' to him before asking a question about the next picture.
4. Do they look at the interlocutor? Is this a good thing? – No, they don't look at the interlocutor and this is a good thing because the interlocutor does not join in the discussion in Part 3.
5. Does the interlocutor ask them questions during the task? – No. The interlocutor will only speak during this part of the test if the students are not performing the task appropriately.
6. Who speaks the most during Part 3? – Giallo speaks most during this part of the test.

7. Do they take turns, or does one person dominate the discussion? – They take turns to speak and initiate discussion. No one dominates the interaction but Ana does not take full advantage of her opportunities to speak.

8. Do they speak about all the pictures? – Yes.

9. Do they reach a joint decision? Does this matter? – No. Ana thinks football matches on the TV and half-price coffees would be good while Giallo prefers the idea of comfortable sofas. This is absolutely fine. Giallo and Ana do not make a decision until they have done the first part of the task and discussed all the pictures. It is important that students don't start to make decisions too early on as this means they will run out of things to say or that they have to go round the visuals again and they then risk repeating themselves.

■ Task Three

1. Play Part 3 on the DVD again. Ask the students to complete the table on the worksheet.

Students would only write short notes but the whole transcript is here to show exactly what each student contributed to the discussion and how they did it.

Answers

Pictures	Ana	Giallo
Live music	Live music in a bar could be good I think. It's attractive for people.	So in the first one they propose music. What do you think about that?
Comfortable sofas	I like also that one with the sofas. It seems to be very relaxing, maybe . . . chatting with your friend . . . like at home.	. . . Yes exactly . . . makes this place comfortable and attractive.
Half-price coffee	Yeah I agree with you.	I think this is one of the best ideas – I mean, one coffee for free, particularly when you open a place, you know it's a good way to . . .
Tables outside	Yeah, this one seems to be good – the terrace – but maybe if you have a good weather . . .	Yes, I don't know here in Cambridge . . . And then if you . . . have just opened a café or a bar maybe it's not a good idea to . . . put some . . . tables outside. I think it's better to concentrate on music or other ideas . . .
TV and football	Yeah, yeah . . . What do you think about football matches? 'Sports'? Yeah me not but most of the people I think – maybe it's a good idea.	Depends on the target . . . of the public that you are interested in. I mean if you are interested in . . . attracting men it's more than good, it's a perfect idea but I don't know. You can tell! I mean would you go in a café with a football match?
Open at night	It's difficult a café at night I think.	Open at night? I don't think in the beginning. Do you agree with me? . . . Yes, it depends until when.
International menu	An international menu – yeah – to attract a lot of people from different countries yeah – I think so.	This is I think also important.

2. Ask the students to discuss what they think Giallo and Ana could do to improve their performance in this part of the test.

Answers

Ana

- It is clear from the above that Ana does not give opinions for all the visuals and this often happens in the live tests.
- Ana does some very positive things in this part of the test. She agrees with Giallo and questions him but she does not contribute fully to the discussion because sometimes she agrees without offering further information (see her contribution on 'half-price coffee') and sometimes gives an opinion without giving reasons (see 'live music'). She asks a question: 'What do you think about football matches?', but having done this she needed to tell Giallo her views about football matches which she fails to do.
- Sometimes her contributions are inadequate: 'It's difficult a café at night I think'. She needs to give reasons why.
- Ana does well in the decision-making phase of the discussion where she contributes more fully and goes into the reasons for her opinions.

Giallo

- Giallo does well in this part of the test. He invites his partner to speak, gives reasons for his opinions, listens to what Ana says and adds to her contributions, sometimes agreeing and sometimes disagreeing with her.
- He takes turns sensitively, sometimes moving the discussion forward by starting to discuss a new picture, or listening to Ana's views and responding to her.
- In the decision-making phase of the discussion he responds to Ana's decision by agreeing with her about one point but disagreeing and making his own decision about the other.
- Giallo could have improved his performance by going into more detail and giving reasons for his opinions about late night opening and the international menu.
- Even when he asked Ana for her views, which is a good thing to do, he should still have remembered to give his own views about the picture before moving on.

■ Useful phrases

Below are some useful phrases which may be helpful for students when doing this task, but students should take care not to overuse them.

Initiating/focusing	So we have to . . . Shall we talk about . . . first? Shall we start with this picture? I think we need to . . . We have to choose . . . What do you think about . . . ?
Opinions/views/ideas	What do you think about . . . ? It seems to me that . . . I think . . . What do you think? From what I know . . . In my opinion . . . As far as I'm concerned . . . Personally speaking, . . . Could I just add that . . . ? If I might come in here . . . Don't you think . . . ? I've heard . . . I'm sure . . .
Agreeing	That's a good point. I think you're right about that. I hadn't (really) thought of that. That's a good idea! That's exactly what I think.
Disagreeing	I see what you mean, but don't you think . . . ? Yes, but isn't it true that . . . ? I'm not so sure about that. Do you think . . . ? I don't really agree with you about that because . . . But do you really think it's a good idea to . . . ? That's a good point but I think . . . because . . .
Concluding	So, what shall we say? So, what do you think? I think this is the best idea because . . . OK. Shall we say . . . ? Do you agree?

1. Students at this level will need to be taught to initiate ideas as well as responding to their partner's ideas. They need to give and justify their opinions and be able to turn-take showing sensitivity to their partner. They should also be able to reach a negotiated conclusion by selecting and evaluating the visuals. It is therefore important to involve students in as much group discussion as possible, giving feedback on individual performance.

2. To deal with issues of turn-taking, make one student in the group responsible for ensuring that everyone gets equal opportunities to speak.

3. To enable less confident students to participate in discussions, give students time to prepare and make notes on the topic chosen for discussion before the discussion begins. They could do this alone or in pairs.

4. Nearer to the time of the exam, give students timed practice of this part of the test so that they get a feel for the length of the discussion. More confident students could be asked to demonstrate a Part 3 task for the class.

5. Encourage students to take opportunities outside the class to improve their knowledge of general issues by reading a newspaper or watching programmes on television such as the news, documentaries or other programmes which involve discussion.

Remind students that:

- they should question each other about the visuals and take it in turns to move the discussion forward by embarking on new pictures

- both students should aim to give their opinions about every picture so that they do not complete the task too quickly. (Many students follow a pattern along the lines of: Student A talks about the first picture, Student B about the second and so on. This often means they get through the visuals too quickly and have to go round them all again which can become repetitive

- they are not penalised for not finding time to talk about all the pictures, nor for running out of time before they have made a final decision

- if they stop before they have spoken for the full 3 minutes, they are unlikely to be able to get full marks for the range of language they have demonstrated

- they are not being assessed on their knowledge of the world, but if they don't express any ideas or opinions, it will be difficult for the examiners to give a fair appraisal of their language ability.

Make sure you know exactly what you have to do before you start to speak. Ask the interlocutor to repeat the instructions if you are not sure.

Don't make your decisions too early in the discussion. Do the first part of the task fully for all the photographs before you make your decisions.

Say as much as you can about a photograph before you move on. This will mean you don't have to go back and talk about the photographs again to fill the time.

Don't worry if you don't have time to make a decision. You won't lose marks for this. What is important is that you speak for the full 3 minutes.

Make sure that you share the interaction with your partner. Sometimes you should start talking about the photograph first and sometimes you should allow your partner to begin.

Share the time with your partner. When you've said what you want to say, ask them a question so that they have the chance to talk.

Listen carefully to what your partner is saying. Can you make a comment about what he or she has said?

It's good to agree and disagree with your partner but **if you disagree make sure you do it in a polite and sensitive way**.

Even though you're speaking to your partner, **don't forget to speak clearly** so that the interlocutor and assessor can hear you.

UNIVERSITY *of* CAMBRIDGE
ESOL Examinations

FCE Speaking test
Teacher's Notes

This worksheet is based on Part 4 of the FCE Speaking test.

■ Task One

1. Ask the students to work with a partner and discuss each question in turn.
   - Would you like to spend time in a café like this? (Ana)
   - Would you like to work in a café? (Giallo)
   - What sorts of restaurants are most popular with visitors in your country? (Giallo – then Ana)
   - What sort of things do people complain about in cafés and restaurants? (Both)
   - Young people usually go to different places to relax than older people. Why do you think that is? (Both)
   - Some people say that going out to relax is a waste of time and money. Do you agree? (Both)

   Give general feedback on how students deal with the questions. Encourage them to extend their answers as much as possible.

2. Play Part 4 on the DVD and ask students to write down who answers each of the questions above. Invite general comments about Giallo's and Ana's performance.

■ Task Two

Play Part 4 again and ask the students to answer the questions on the worksheet.

Answers

1. Does the interlocutor ask each candidate the same questions? – The interlocutor can sometimes ask the same question to each candidate individually as in Question 3.
2. Does the interlocutor ask candidates to answer questions individually, or discuss them together? – The interlocutor can ask questions individually or ask both candidates to discuss the questions together. Many interlocutors will ask candidates individual and joint questions.
3. Do the candidates only speak when asked by the interlocutor? – The candidates answer the questions they are asked. They do not interrupt each other when individual questions have been asked, but when questions are addressed to both of them they talk together naturally and extend their answers fully showing an ability to turn-take without help from the interlocutor.
4. Do the candidates always extend their answers? – Yes, they both do well in this part of the test. Ana needed to give a more extended response to Question 1.
5. How do candidates extend their answers? – By giving reasons and details about their ideas. By responding to each other and questioning each other when questions are addressed to both of them.
6. How does the interlocutor finish the test? – 'Thank you. That is the end of the test.'

■ Task Three

1. What is the difference between the direct questions candidates are asked in Part 1 and those in Part 4? Ask the students to complete the sentences on their worksheet with the information from the box.

personal information	both candidates	an individual candidate	opinions

Answers

a) Part 1 questions ask for **personal information** but Part 4 questions ask for **opinions**.
b) Part 1 questions are addressed to **an individual candidate** but Part 4 questions can be addressed to **both candidates**.

2. Ask the students to decide, using the information above, which of the questions in the box are from Part 1 and which are from Part 4.

Answers

Questions	Which part?
How important is it to have places where nature is protected? (Why?)	Part 4
What do you like about living in (candidate's country/home town)?	Part 1
What sort of job are you hoping to do in the future? (Why?)	Part 1
Which do you think is more important, trying to do something or being successful? (Why?)	Part 4
What do you like doing in your free time? (Why do you enjoy doing that?)	Part 1
What is the difference between a friend and a best friend? (Why?)	Part 4
Do you think it's better to live in one place all your life, or to live in lots of different places? (Why?)	Part 4
How often do you go away on holiday? (Where do you/would you like to go?)	Part 1
Do you judge people by what they say or how they look? (Why?)	Part 4
Where would you take someone for a day out where you live?	Part 1
Does good entertainment have to cost a lot of money? (Why/Why not?)	Part 4

■ Useful phrases

Below are some useful phrases which may be helpful for students when doing this part of the test, but students should take care not to overuse them.

Offering a tentative opinion	I'm not sure . . . Probably . . . Perhaps . . . Maybe . . . It's very difficult . . ., but I think . . . It's not something I feel very strongly about, but . . .
Developing the discussion	I'd like to add something . . . There's something else I'd like to say . . . I couldn't have put it better myself.
Offering a strong opinion	Actually, I feel quite strongly that . . . I'm quite certain that . . . I know for a fact that . . . I really don't think it is right that . . .
Expressing agreement	Could I just add that . . . ? Exactly!

1. Part 4 is a continuation of Part 3. Candidates should be prepared to:
   - offer an opinion
   - extend their responses
   - agree/disagree with their partner
   - add to or extend their partner's response
   - question their partner
   - allow their partner to speak for a similar amount of time

2. Parts 3 and 4 both involve discussion. Therefore the suggestions for Part 3 of the test will also be helpful for Part 4.

3. Give students practice of thinking on the spot. Provide a 5–10-minute slot during the lesson for question practice. Start by asking students three or four questions and giving them preparation time to think up a response. Invite some of the students to share their responses. Tell them that they must say something, even if the question is difficult, and that they should say as much as possible if they find the question easy. Gradually cut the preparation time down until students feel confident enough to answer straight away. Students often lack confidence in this part of the test, thinking that what they have to say might not be good enough. Frequent practice and the opportunity to hear other students' responses will build their confidence in this part of the test.

4. Try to cover a range of topics and gradually increase the difficulty of the questions asked. The following topics are given as examples:
   - education
   - holidays
   - past and present
   - travel and transport
   - jobs
   - the environment
   - technology
   - the future

Listen carefully to the questions and try to answer confidently.

Always try to answer the questions fully. When you tell the examiner what you think try to tell the examiner **why** you think that as well.

Sometimes the interlocutor will ask you a question and sometimes you will be asked to discuss something with your partner. If you're asked to discuss something with your partner, **listen carefully to what your partner is saying** and decide whether you agree or disagree. Make sure, if you disagree, that you do it politely.

Be sensitive. Don't talk for too long without giving your partner or the interlocutor a chance to speak.

UNIVERSITY *of* CAMBRIDGE
ESOL Examinations

FCE Speaking test
Teacher's Notes

SUPPLEMENTARY
WORKSHEET

■ How we assess speaking for FCE

Candidates are assessed on their own individual performance and not in relation to each other, according to the following four analytical criteria: grammar and vocabulary, discourse management, pronunciation and interactive communication. These criteria are interpreted at FCE level. Assessment is based on performance in the whole test and is not related to performance in particular parts of the test.

Both examiners assess the candidates. The assessor applies detailed analytical scales, and the interlocutor applies a global achievement scale, which is based on the analytical scale.

■ Analytical scales

Grammar and vocabulary

This refers to the accurate and appropriate use of a range of grammatical forms and vocabulary. Performance is viewed in terms of the overall effectiveness of the language used in spoken interaction.

Discourse management

This refers to the candidate's ability to link utterances together to form coherent speech, without undue hesitation. The utterances should be relevant to the tasks, and should be arranged logically to develop the themes or arguments required by the tasks.

Pronunciation

This refers to the candidate's ability to produce comprehensible utterances to fulfil the task requirements. This includes stress and intonation as well as individual sounds. Examiners put themselves in the position of a non-ESOL specialist and assess the overall impact of the pronunciation and the degree of effort required to understand the candidate.

Interactive communication

This refers to the candidate's ability to take an active part in the development of the discourse. This requires an ability to participate in the range of interactive situations in the test and to develop discussions on a range of topics by initiating and responding appropriately. This also refers to the deployment of strategies to maintain interaction at an appropriate level throughout the test so that the tasks can be fulfilled.

■ Global achievement scale

This refers to the candidate's overall performance in dealing with the tasks in the four separate parts of the FCE Speaking test. The global mark is an independent impression mark which reflects the assessment of the candidate's performance from the interlocutor's perspective.

■ FCE typical minimum adequate performance

The candidate develops the interaction with contributions which are mostly coherent and extended when dealing with the FCE-level tasks. Grammar is mostly accurate and vocabulary appropriate. Utterances are understood with very little strain on the listener.

Please note:

Candidates cannot pass or fail any individual paper. The candidate's grade for the examination is based on their total score from all five papers.

■ Assessment task

Answers

Grammar and vocabulary	Use a range of structures. Try not to make basic mistakes. Try to use interesting words, not just the same ones all the time. Try to be precise in the words you use.
Discourse management	Try to connect your ideas together clearly. Make sure that you speak for an appropriate length of time.
Pronunciation	Don't worry too much if you have an accent, but try to speak very clearly so that your partner and the interlocutor can understand what you are saying. Think about the person listening to you – how can you help them to understand what you are saying?
Interactive communication	Participate in all parts of the test. Remember to start discussions as well as responding to what your partner says. Give your opinions with confidence and try not to hesitate for too long before you speak.

FCE Speaking test
Student Worksheets

This section contains the six Student Worksheets for FCE:
- Introductory Worksheet – provides an introduction to the FCE Speaking test as a whole
- Worksheet 1 – based on Part 1 of the FCE Speaking test
- Worksheet 2 – based on Part 2 of the FCE Speaking test
- Worksheet 3 – based on Part 3 of the FCE Speaking test
- Worksheet 4 – based on Part 4 of the FCE Speaking test
- Supplementary Worksheet – explains how the FCE Speaking test is assessed.

The Student Worksheet pages of this book are photocopiable and you can also print copies from the Student Worksheets file on the DVD. For your class you will also need:
- the DVD
- for Parts 2 and 3, the candidate visuals. You can find one set of these inside the front and back covers of this book. There is also a file on the DVD with the candidate visuals if you want to print more copies and have access to a colour printer.

■ Aims of the DVD and worksheets

- to raise your awareness of the format of the FCE Speaking test
- to focus your attention on techniques that will improve your performance
- to provide opportunities for you to practise the language used in the different parts of the test.

Please note:

The DVD and worksheets are not intended as a forum for discussing grades. Although in certain questions we are asking you to look at the candidates' performance, it is with a view to improving your own performance and not for you to grade the candidates on the DVD.

The FCE Speaking test on the DVD has been produced for teaching purposes only and is not a live exam. There are therefore, no grades available.

Some of the answers to the activities in the worksheets cannot be found on the DVD.

Student's Introductory Worksheet

Before watching the DVD, test your knowledge of the FCE Speaking test by completing as much of the following worksheet as you can. You can find some of the information you need on the Candidate Support site at

www.candidates.CambridgeESOL.org/cs/Help_with_exams/General_English/FCE

and in the *Information for Candidates* booklet which you can download.

■ Task One: general information about the FCE Speaking test

Fill in the missing information:

1. Length: _____ minutes

2. Normal format: _____ candidates and _____ examiners

3. Number of parts: _____

4. The Speaking test is worth _____% of the whole FCE exam (all papers).

■ Task Two: what happens in the FCE Speaking test

Complete the table with the missing information from the box below.

• leads a discussion • exchanges views and opinions • asks individual direct questions	• expresses opinions through comparing • gives personal information • initiates discussion

Parts	Timing	What the interlocutor does	What a candidate does
1. Interview	3 minutes	_____ _____	_____ _____
2. Individual long turn	4 minutes	asks each candidate to talk about two visuals for 1 minute	_____ _____
3. Collaborative task	3 minutes	asks candidates to talk together using visual prompts	exchanges ideas and opinions, makes suggestions, agrees, disagrees, and _____
4. Discussion on topics related to Part 3	4 minutes	_____ _____	_____ _____

■ Task Three: about the FCE Speaking test

Read the following statements and write 'True' or 'False' next to each one:

1. You can choose to take the test in a pair or a group of three. _____

2. The assessor asks you questions during the test. _____

3. Only the assessor awards marks. _____

4. You are given your marks at the end of the test. _____

5. You might not know your partner. _____

6. You are not tested on your general knowledge. _____

7. In Part 1, you ask your partner questions. _____

8. In Part 2, if your partner runs out of things to say you can help. _____

9. The questions are written at the top of the page in Parts 2 and 3. _____

10. You should interact with your partner in both Parts 3 and 4. _____

 Check your answers with a partner. Then watch the whole Speaking test on the DVD to see if you were right.

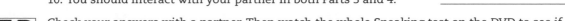

This worksheet is based on Part 1 of the FCE Speaking test.

■ Task One

1. Read the questions below. Work with a partner and ask and answer them in turn.
   - Where are you from?
   - What do you like about living in (partner's country/UK)?
   - Do you find it easy to study where you live? (Why?/Why not?)
   - Is there something you'd really like to learn about? (Why would you like to learn about it?)
   - Which area of (candidate's country) would you like to get to know better?
   - What's the most interesting place you've visited near here? (Why do you think it's interesting?)
   - How much TV do you watch in a week? (Do you think this is too much?) (Why?/Why not?)
   - Do you use the internet to learn new things? (What sort of things do you learn about?)

 2. Now watch Ana and Giallo do Part 1 on the DVD. How were your answers different from theirs?

■ Task Two

 1. Watch Part 1 on the DVD again and make notes in the table below:

What does Ana say about . . .	What does Giallo say about . . .
Madrid when she answers question 1?	Perugia when he answers question 1?
Madrid when she answers question 2?	living in the UK?
the area of her country she'd like to know better?	studying?
the most interesting place she's visited?	how much TV he watches?
using the internet to learn new things?	

Compare your notes with other students in the group.

2. Watch Part 1 on the DVD again if necessary and then discuss these questions:
   - Which questions do Giallo and Ana answer well?
   - Which questions could they have answered better?
   - Who do you think gave the best answers in Part 1 of the test? Why?

■ Task Three

1. Look at the topic areas below. Think of two questions to ask your partner in each area.

   - sports
   - leisure interests
   - work and study
   - family
   - travel and holidays
   - entertainment
   - experiences
   - daily life
   - jobs/studies/education
   - the area where they live
   - likes and dislikes
   - future plans

   You can write your questions in the box below if you like.

Topic area	My questions
_____	1. _____ 2. _____
_____	1. _____ 2. _____
_____	1. _____ 2. _____
_____	1. _____ 2. _____
_____	1. _____ 2. _____
_____	1. _____ 2. _____

2. Then practise in pairs or small groups, taking turns to ask your partner(s) your questions, and answer their questions.

This worksheet is based on Part 2 of the FCE Speaking test.

■ Task One: focus on Ana

1. Watch the beginning of Part 2 on the DVD and listen carefully to the interlocutor's instructions to Ana. Write the missing information in the box below.

> *Interlocutor:* Ana, it's your turn first. Here are your photographs. They show_____
>
> _____ .
>
> I'd like you to compare the photographs and say_____
>
> _____ .

2. What question do you think the interlocutor will ask Giallo? Write your idea in the box below.

> *Interlocutor:* Giallo,_____ ?

3. Now work with a partner and take it in turns to do Ana's task. Then discuss these questions with your partner:
   - Did you speak for a minute?
   - Did you compare two pictures in an organised way and answer the second part of the task?

4. Now watch Ana do the task on the DVD and compare your performance with hers. Discuss these questions with your partner:
   - Why does Ana find it hard to do this task?
   - How does your question for Giallo (above) compare with the question the interlocutor asks Giallo?

■ Task Two: focus on Giallo

1. Watch the next part of Part 2 on the DVD and listen carefully to the interlocutor's instructions to Giallo. Write the missing information in the box below.

> *Interlocutor:* Giallo, here are your photographs. They show _____
>
> _____ .
>
> I'd like you to compare the photographs and say_____
>
> _____ .

2. What question do you think the interlocutor will ask Ana? Write your idea in the box below.

> *Interlocutor:* Ana, _____ ?

3. Now work with a partner and take it in turns to do Giallo's task. Then discuss these questions:
   - Did you speak for a minute?
   - Did you remember to answer the second part of the task?
   - Did you look at the questions on your sheet to remind yourself of what you had to say?

4. Now watch Giallo do the task on the DVD and compare your performance with his. Discuss these questions with your partner:
   - Did Giallo do anything that you didn't do?
   - How does your question for Ana (on the previous page) compare with the question the interlocutor asks Ana?

■ Task Three

1. Watch the whole of Part 2 again, and complete the table below.

What do they say . . .	Ana	Giallo
What do they say about the first picture?		
What do they say about the second picture?		
What do they say when they compare the pictures?		
What do they say when they answer the second part of the task?		
Do they give an appropriate response to the listening candidate question?		

2. Who does the task best, Ana or Giallo? _____

   Why?_____

   _____

This worksheet is based on Part 3 of the FCE Speaking test.

■ Task One

1. Watch the beginning of Part 3 on the DVD and listen carefully to the interlocutor's instructions. Write the missing information in the box below.

> *Interlocutor:* Now I'd like you to talk about something together for about 3 minutes.
>
> I'd like you to imagine that a local café wants to attract more people. Here are some of the suggestions they're considering.
>
> First, talk to each other about _____
>
> _____ .
>
> Then decide _____
>
> _____ .

2. Work with a partner and do the task above. Make sure that you spend 3 minutes discussing all the pictures.

3. Discuss these questions with your partner:
   - Did you have time to discuss all the pictures?
   - Did you have something to say about all the pictures?
   - Did you find any pictures easy or difficult to talk about?
   - Did you reach a decision too early and leave yourselves with nothing else to talk about?

4. Now watch Ana and Giallo do the task on the DVD and compare your performance with theirs.

■ Task Two

Watch Ana and Giallo doing this part of the test on the DVD again and answer the following questions:

1. Who starts the discussion and how?

   _____

2. Who responds the most and how?

   _____

3. Do they seem interested in each other and what they are saying?

   _____

4. Do they look at the interlocutor? Is this a good thing?

   _____

5. Does the interlocutor ask them questions during the task?

   _____

6. Who speaks the most during Part 3?

   _____

7. Do they take turns, or does one person dominate the discussion?

_____

8. Do they speak about all the pictures?

_____

9. Do they reach a joint decision? Does this matter?

_____

■ Task Three

1. Now watch Part 3 of the test again. What do Giallo and Ana say about each of the pictures? Make short notes in the box below.

Pictures	Ana	Giallo
Live music		
Comfortable sofas		
Half-price coffee		
Tables outside		
TV and football		
Open at night		
International menu		

2. What do you think Giallo and Ana could do to improve their performance in this part of the test? Note down some other language you think they could have used to do the following:

Language to:	My examples
turn-take	
initiate discussion	
ask for and give opinions	
conclude/ summarise	

This worksheet is based on Part 4 of the FCE Speaking test.

■ Task One

1. Here are six questions related to the Part 3 task. Work with a partner and discuss each one in turn.
   - Would you like to spend time in a café like this?
   - Would you like to work in a café?
   - What sorts of restaurants are most popular with visitors in your country?
   - What sort of things do people complain about in cafés and restaurants?
   - Young people usually go to different places to relax than older people. Why do you think that is?
   - Some people say that going out to relax is a waste of time and money. Do you agree?

2. Now watch Ana and Giallo do Part 4 on the DVD. Make a note of who answers each question and how well you think Giallo and Ana answer the questions. Compare your answers with theirs.

■ Task Two

Watch Part 4 again and answer the following questions:

1. Does the interlocutor ask each candidate the same questions?

   _____

2. Does the interlocutor ask candidates to answer questions individually, or discuss them together?

   _____

3. Do the candidates only speak when asked by the interlocutor?

   _____

4. Do the candidates always extend their answers?

   _____

5. How do candidates extend their answers?

   _____

6. How does the interlocutor finish the test?

   _____

■ Task Three

1. What is the difference between the direct questions in Part 1 and the direct questions in Part 4? Complete the two sentences below with the information from the box.

personal information	both candidates	an individual candidate	opinions

   a) Part 1 questions ask for _____ but Part 4 questions ask for _____ .

   b) Part 1 questions are addressed to _____ but Part 4 questions can be addressed to _____ .

2. Using the information on the previous page, decide which of the questions in the box below are from Part 1 and which are from Part 4. Write your answers in the boxes on the right.

Questions	Which part?
How important is it to have places where nature is protected? (Why?)	
What do you like about living in (candidate's country/home town)?	
What sort of job are you hoping to do in the future? (Why?)	
Which do you think is more important, trying to do something or being successful? (Why?)	
What do you like doing in your free time? (Why do you enjoy doing that?)	
What is the difference between a friend and a best friend? (Why?)	
Do you think it's better to live in one place all your life, or to live in lots of different places? (Why?)	
How often do you go away on holiday? (Where do you/would you like to go?)	
Do you judge people by what they say or how they look? (Why?)	
Where would you take someone for a day out where you live?	
Does good entertainment have to cost a lot of money? (Why/Why not?)	

This worksheet helps you understand how we assess your speaking for FCE.

■ Assessment task

Here is some advice for getting good marks in each section of the assessment criteria.
Put each piece of advice into the correct box.

- Use a range of structures.
- Remember to start discussions as well as responding to what your partner says.
- Try to use interesting words, not just the same ones all the time.
- Try to connect your ideas together clearly.
- Think about the person listening to you – how can you help them to understand what you are saying?
- Try to be precise in the words you use.
- Give your opinions with confidence and try not to hesitate for too long before you speak.
- Try not to make basic mistakes.
- Participate in all parts of the test.
- Make sure that you speak for an appropriate length of time.
- Don't worry too much if you have an accent, but try to speak very clearly so that your partner and the interlocutor can understand what you are saying.

Grammar and vocabulary	
Discourse management	
Pronunciation	
Interactive communication	

Dos and Don'ts checklist

■ Throughout the test

Do listen carefully to instructions given and questions asked throughout the test and focus your answers appropriately.

Do ask for clarification from the interlocutor if you are not sure what you have been asked.

Do speak clearly so that both examiners can hear you.

Do make use of opportunities to speak in all parts of the test, and extend your answers where appropriate.

Don't worry about being interrupted by the interlocutor. It's important that the interlocutor keeps to the correct timing throughout the test.

■ Part 1

Don't prepare long responses in advance. You are unlikely to answer questions correctly.

Don't just answer yes or no as you will not demonstrate a range of language.

Do extend your answers appropriately by giving reasons or examples.

Do remember that these questions are asking for information about you and not so much about your opinions.

■ Part 2

Don't just describe the photographs. Follow the interlocutor's instructions and answer the question as this will help you produce language at the right level.

Do use the written prompts on the paper to help you remember the task.

Do give a short confident answer to the question about your partner's pictures.

Don't interrupt your partner's long turn.

Don't worry about being interrupted by the interlocutor when you have spoken for a minute.

Don't try to give your views during your partner's long turn.

■ Part 3

Do use the written prompts on the paper to help you remember the task.

Do respond to what your partner says before making new suggestions.

Do be sensitive to turn-taking.

Do talk about each picture together in detail before moving on to the next.

Don't try to dominate your partner or interrupt them in an abrupt way.

Don't simply respond to what your partner says all the time. Be prepared to initiate discussion by asking questions and developing topics.

Don't worry if you disagree with your partner. As long as you are polite and not overbearing this is all part of interactive communication.

Don't make your decision too early – it should come at the end of your discussion.

■ Part 4

Do try to give full answers wherever possible – give reasons and examples for what you think.

Do discuss answers with your partner when invited to do so by the interlocutor.

Do remember that you should give your opinions but there is no 'right' answer – you are assessed on your language not your ideas.

Don't worry if you disagree with your partner's ideas – you can show your language skills by disagreeing politely and giving reasons.

NOTES

NOTES

- How successful might these suggestions be?
- Which two would attract most people?

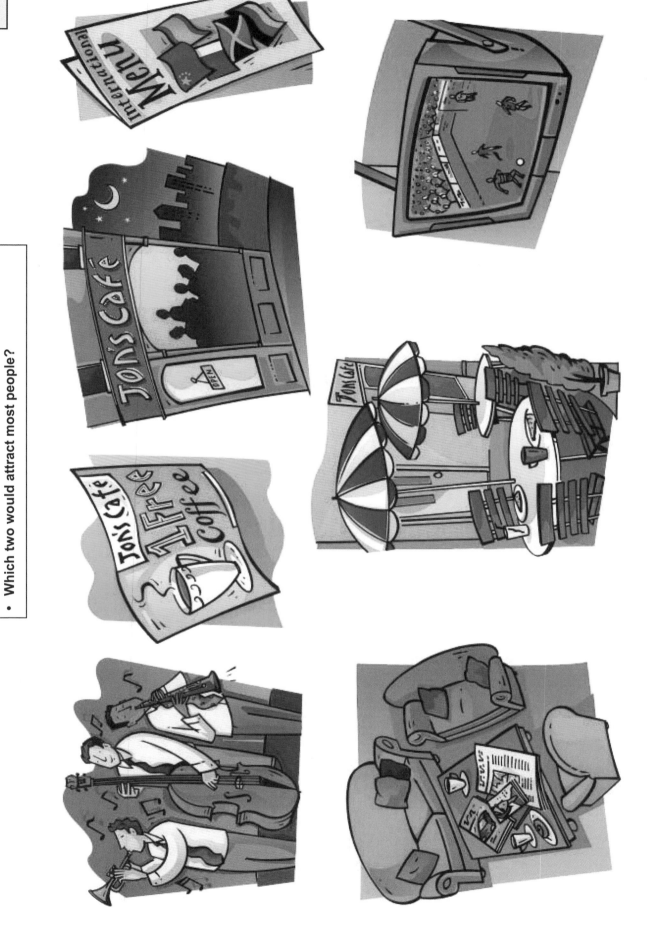